a gift for

Pam

"One of the
Kindest people I know!"

from

love
your sister ♡
Wendy

12 11 10 9 8 7 6 5

Edited and pictures selected by Helen Exley.
Printed in China

Exley Publications Ltd, 16 Chalk Hill, Watford,
Herts WD19 4BG, UK.
Exley Publications LLC, 232 Madison Avenue, Suite 1409,
NY 10016, USA.

www.Hallmark.com

WORDS ON *kindness*

GIFT BOOKS

Selected for Hallmark by Helen Exley

■EXLEY

BOK5043

THE CENTER
OF HUMAN NATURE
IS ROOTED
IN TEN THOUSAND
ORDINARY
ACTS OF KINDNESS
THAT DEFINE
OUR DAYS.

STEPHEN JAY GOULD

No act of kindness,
no matter how small,
is ever wasted.

A E S O P

It is the greatest
of all mistakes
to do nothing
because
you can only
do little.

SYDNEY SMITH

KINDNESS

IS GIVEN SO SOFTLY,

SO GENTLY,

FALLING

LIKE TINY SEEDS

ALONG OUR PATHS —

AND BRIGHTENING

THEM

WITH FLOWERS.

PAM BROWN,
b.1928

WHEN YOU
CARRY OUT ACTS
OF KINDNESS
YOU GET
A WONDERFUL FEELING
INSIDE.
IT IS AS THOUGH
SOMETHING INSIDE
YOUR BODY
RESPONDS
AND SAYS, YES,
THIS IS HOW
I OUGHT TO FEEL.

RABBI HAROLD KUSHNER

Be kind – everyone you meet
is fighting a hard battle.

JOHN WATSON

When I was going through
a very difficult time,
someone called me up
and played piano music
for me on my
answering machine.
It made me feel very loved,
and I never discovered
who did it.

THE EDITORS OF
CONARI PRESS,
FROM "THE PRACTICE
OF KINDNESS"

Throw out the lifeline,
throw out the lifeline,
Someone is sinking today.

EDWARD SMITH UFFORD

Giving
is so often thought of
in terms of the things
we give,
but our greatest giving
is of our time,
and kindness,
and even comfort for
those who need it.
We look on these gifts
as unimportant —
until we need them.

JOYCE SEQUICHIE HIFLER

A PERSON'S

TRUE WEALTH

IS THE GOOD

HE OR SHE DOES

IN THE WORLD.

MOHAMMED

Guard well within yourself
that treasure, kindness.
Know how to give
without hesitation,
how to lose without regret,
how to acquire
without meanness.

GEORGE SAND
(AURORE DUPIN, BARONNE DUDEVANT)
(1804-1876)

We should give as we would
receive, cheerfully, quickly,
and without hesitation;
for there is no grace in a
benefit that sticks
to the fingers.

SENECA
(4B.C.-65A.D.)

Those
who bring sunshine
into the lives
of others
cannot keep it
from themselves.

JAMES M. BARRIE
(1860-1937)

When a person does
a good deed
when he or she
didn't have to,
God looks down and smiles
and says,
"For this moment alone,
it was worth
creating the world."

THE TALMUD

When a blind man
carries a lame man,
both go forward.

SWEDISH PROVERB

It is one of the most
beautiful compensations
of life that no man
can sincerely try to help
another without
helping himself.

RALPH WALDO EMERSON
(1803-1882)

One of the most difficult
things to give away
is kindness, for it is
usually returned.

MARK ORTMAN

What value
has compassion
that does not
take its object
in its arms?

ANTOINE
DE SAINT-EXUPÉRY
(1900-1944)

The ocean,
king of
mountains
and the mighty
continents
are not
heavy burdens
to bear when
compared
to the burden
of not
repaying
the world's
kindness.

THE BUDDHA
(c.563-c.483B.C.)

The Sufis advise us to speak
only after our words
have managed to pass through
three gates.
At the first gate,
we ask ourselves,
"Are these words true?"
If so, we let them pass on;
if not, back they go.
At the second gate,
we ask, "Are they necessary?"
At the last gate, we ask,
"Are they kind?"

EKNATH EASWARAN

If I can stop one heart
from breaking,
I shall not live in vain:
If I can ease one life
the aching,
Or cool one pain,
Or help one fainting robin
Unto his nest again,
I shall not live in vain.

EMILY DICKINSON
(1830-1886)

One kind word
can warm
three winter months.

JAPANESE PROVERB

The greatest comfort
of my old age,
and that which gives me
the highest satisfaction, is
the pleasing remembrance
of the many benefits
and friendly offices
I have done to others.

CATO (4TH CENTURY)

If, at the end,
all that can be said
of you is that you were
kind — it is enough.

PETER GRAY

Nobody
could make
a greater mistake
than he who
did nothing
because he could
only do a little.

EDMUND BURKE

Even the smallest act
of kindness says
"I care", says "You matter",
says "I thought of you."

JENNY DE VRIES,
b.1915

Wise sayings often fall
on barren ground;
but a kind word is never
thrown away.

SIR ARTHUR HELPS

KINDNESS
IS MORE IMPORTANT
THAN WISDOM,
AND THE RECOGNITION
OF THIS
IS THE BEGINNING
OF WISDOM.

THEODORE
ISAAC
RUBIN

How often it is difficult to
be wisely charitable —
to do good without multiplying
the sources of evil.
To give alms is nothing
unless you give thought also.
It is written, not "blessed is
he that feedeth the poor,"
but "blessed is he that
considereth the poor."
A little thought
and a little kindness
are often worth more
than a great deal of money.

JOHN RUSKIN (1819-1900)

Even as a mother
protects with her life
Her child, her only child,
So with a boundless heart
Should one cherish all
living beings;
Radiating kindness
over the entire world.

THE BUDDHA
(c.563-c.483B.C.)

Kindness
in words creates
confidence.
Kindness in thinking
creates profoundness.
Kindness in giving
creates love.

LAO-TZU
(6TH CENTURY B.C.)

Never, if possible
lie down at night
without
being able to say:
"I have made
one human being
at least a little wiser,
or a little better
this day."

CHARLES KINGSLEY

(1819-1875)

... one of the things we have learned
in our sobriety is the only way
we can keep what we have, or feeling good
about ourselves, is to give it away.

HAROLD BELMONT

Kindness is within
the gift of the very
poor, the wretched,
the despised. It is the
true test of worth.

PAM BROWN, *b*.1928

Kindness makes
the difference between
passion and caring.
Kindness is tenderness,
kindness is love, perhaps
greater than love...
kindness is goodwill,
kindness says "I want
you to be happy."

RANDOLPH RAY

The good feelings we get from
doing kind things for others are
often greater than what we do.
Self-gratification comes from giving
freely and fully out of love and the

*desire to share. Sharing and doing
kind deeds are not done with
expectations; they are given freely
from the heart.
We give because it feels natural
and right. We have taken our
minds off our own troubles.
Self-pity and self-isolation no
longer dominate our thoughts.
We give for the sheer joy of giving
without the need for recognition.*

BRYAN ROBINSON

If you have not often
felt the joy
of doing a kind act,
you have neglected much,
and most of all yourself.

A. NEILEN

When someone does
something, applaud!
That will make two
people happy.

SAMUEL GOLDWYN

If you want
happiness
for an hour —
take a nap.
If you want
happiness
for a day —
go fishing....
If you want
happiness
for a lifetime —
help someone else.

Do not keep the alabaster
boxes of your love and
tenderness sealed up,
until your friends are dead.
Fill their lives with sweetness.
Speak approving, cheering
words while their ears can
hear them and while their
hearts can be thrilled
and made happier by them.
The kind things you mean
to say when they are gone,
say them before they go.

ANONYMOUS

EVERYTHING
THAT IS NOT GIVEN
IS LOST.

I N D I A N
P R O V E R B

Each
human creature
is alone —
but acts of
kindness
take away
our loneliness,
for we
discover
that others
are concerned
for us.

PAM BROWN,
b. 1928

Kindness is the golden chain
by which society is bound together.

JOHANN
WOLFGANG VON GOETHE
(1749-1832)

We are all crowded
together on a very
small planet.
A difficult family.
A collection of
close relatives.
Let us be kind
to one another.

PAM BROWN,
b.1928

Always
be a little kinder
than necessary.

JAMES M. BARRIE
(1860-1937)

The kindness

I *have longest remembered*

has been of this sort,

the sort unsaid;

so far behind

the speaker's lips

that almost it already

lay in my heart.

It *did not have far to go*

to be communicated.

HENRY DAVID THOREAU

(1817-1862)

I expect to pass through
life but once. If therefore,
there be any kindness
I can show, or any good
thing I can do
to any fellow being,
let me do it now, and not
defer or neglect it,
as I shall not pass
this way again.

WILLIAM PENN
(1644-1718)

Human beings who leave
behind them
no great achievements,
but only a sequence of
small kindnesses,
have not had wasted lives.

CHARLOTTE GRAY,
b.1937

Kind words can be short
and easy to speak,
but their echoes are endless.

MOTHER TERESA
(1910-1997)

ACKNOWLEDGEMENTS: The publishers are grateful for permission to reproduce copyright material. Whilst every effort has been made to trace copyright holders, the publishers would be pleased to hear from any not here acknowledged. PAM BROWN: Used by permission. EDITORS OF CONARI PRESS: Extract from *The Random Acts of Kindness*, copyright © 1993 by The Editors of Conari Press. JOYCE SEQUICHIE HIFLER: Extract reprinted with permission of Council Oak Books from *A Cherokee Feast of Days*, by Joyce Sequichie Hifler; copyright © 1992 by Joyce Sequichie Hifler. BRYAN ROBINSON: Extract from *Time for Thoughtfulness* by Ruth Fishel © 1994 Ruth Fishel. Reprinted with permission of Health Communications, Inc.

PICTURE CREDITS: Exley Publications would like to thank the following organizations and individuals for permission to reproduce their pictures. Whilst every effort has been made to trace copyright holders, the publishers would be pleased to hear from any not here acknowledged. Allied Artists, AISA, Art Resource (AR), Artworks, Bridgeman Art Library (BAL), Chris Beetles Gallery, Edimedia (EDM), Fine Art Photographic Library (FAP), Image Bank, Sotheby's, Statenskonstmuseer, Stockholm (SKM), Superstock (SS).
Cover, pages 8/9 and 64/65: © 1995 Diana Armfield, BAL; title page: © 1997 Daniel Mark Duffy, *Sunset*, Artworks; page 7: Artist unknown, *Basket of Geraniums*, SS; page 10: © 1997 Kevin MacPherson, *Rose Garden &*

ACKNOWLEDGEMENTS: The publishers are grateful for permission to reproduce copyright material. Whilst every effort has been made to trace copyright holders, the publishers would be pleased to hear from any not here acknowledged. PAM BROWN: Used by permission. EDITORS OF CONARI PRESS: Extract from *The Random Acts of Kindness*, copyright © 1993 by The Editors of Conari Press. JOYCE SEQUICHIE HIFLER: Extract reprinted with permission of Council Oak Books from *A Cherokee Feast of Days*, by Joyce Sequichie Hifler; copyright © 1992 by Joyce Sequichie Hifler. BRYAN ROBINSON: Extract from *Time for Thoughtfulness* by Ruth Fishel © 1994 Ruth Fishel. Reprinted with permission of Health Communications, Inc.

PICTURE CREDITS: Exley Publications would like to thank the following organizations and individuals for permission to reproduce their pictures. Whilst every effort has been made to trace copyright holders, the publishers would be pleased to hear from any not here acknowledged. Allied Artists, AISA, Art Resource (AR), Artworks, Bridgeman Art Library (BAL), Chris Beetles Gallery, Edimedia (EDM), Fine Art Photographic Library (FAP), Image Bank, Sotheby's, Statenskonstmuseer, Stockholm (SKM), Superstock (SS).
Cover, title-page and endpapers: © 2001 Hallmark Gift Books; page 7: Artist unknown, *Basket of Geraniums*, SS; pages 8/9 and 64/65: © 1995 Diana Armfield, BAL; page